The I
Leonardo da Vinci

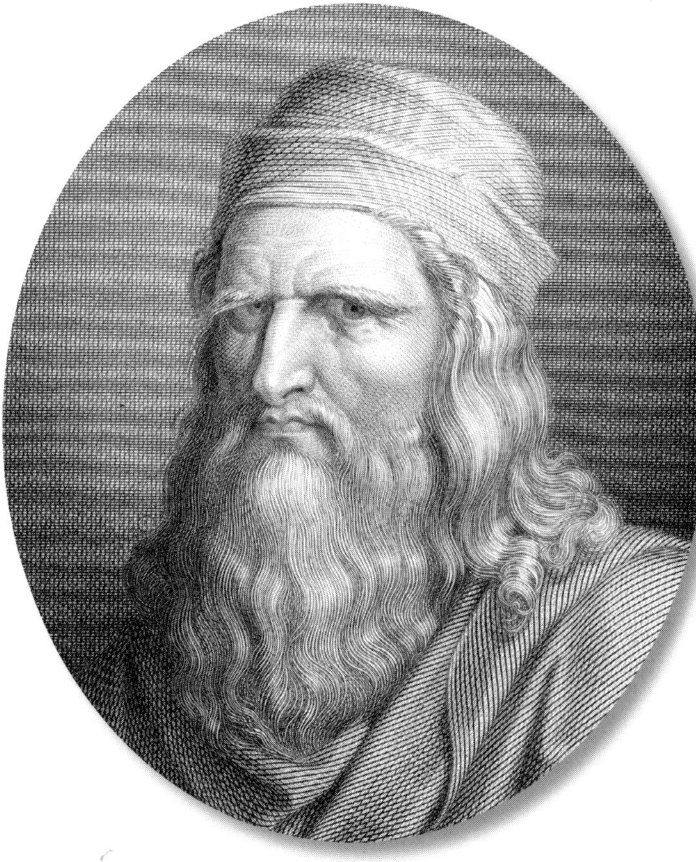

by Ann Weil

BOSTON

Leonardo da Vinci loved to learn about the world.

Leonardo da Vinci was a famous artist. He painted the *Mona Lisa.* He was also a good singer and musician. And he was a scientist and inventor, a person who makes things.

Leonardo lived in Europe about 500 years ago. He did not go to school. He was still one of the smartest people of his time. Some people today say he was one of the smartest people of all time.

Leonardo was very interested in the world around him. Nature was his favorite thing to study. He studied plants, animals, and the human body and how it works. He wanted to understand everything.

Leonardo had a different way of learning from other people of his time. He started with an idea. Then he tested his idea. He wrote down what happened. Leonardo was one of the first people to work this way. This is how scientists work today.

Leonardo wrote his ideas in notebooks. He also made drawings of things he saw. He filled the pages with writing, drawings, and lists. Some of these pages are in museums now. However, many pages were lost.

The notebooks have many drawings of the human body. Leonardo used what he learned about the human body in his paintings. His paintings looked more real than paintings by other artists of his time.

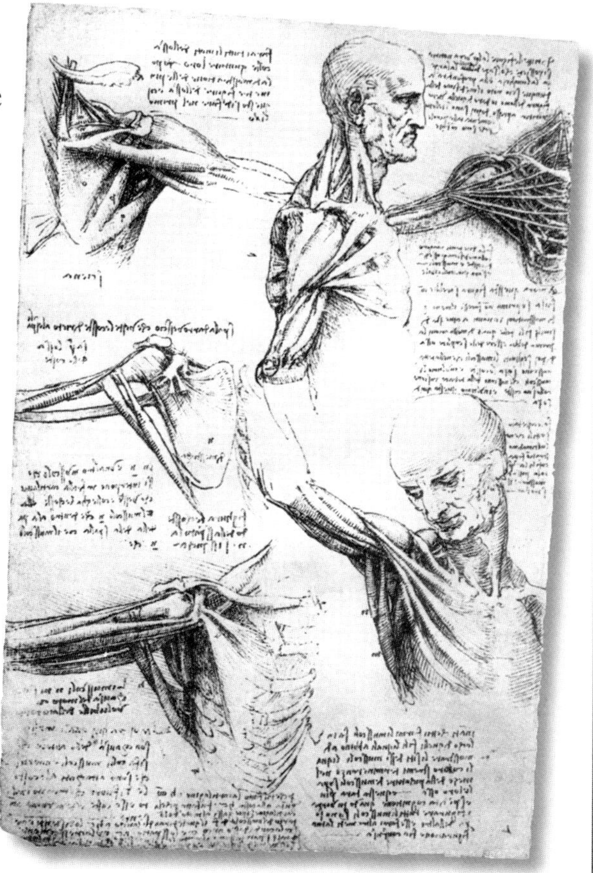

Leonardo made drawings of the human body.

Machines

Leonardo also invented machines. He used what he learned about the human body to help him. He drew pictures of these machines in his notebooks.

Machines help people do work. They make work faster and easier. We use machines every day. There are machines at home, at school, and almost everywhere we look.

We use machines to go from place to place. Cars, airplanes, trains, and bicycles are all machines.

These are just some of the many machines people use every day.

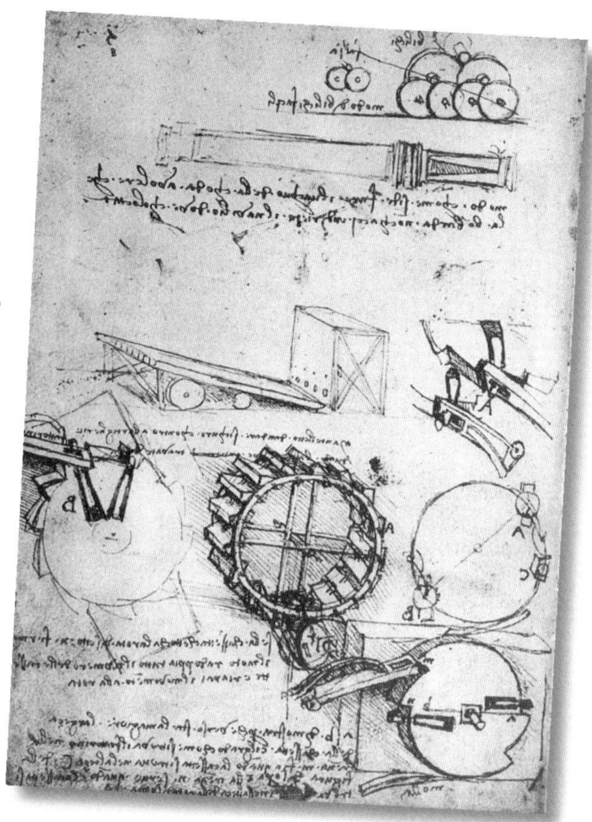

Leonardo kept a notebook of drawings. He combined simple machines in new and exciting ways to create more complex machines.

Some machines are very simple. A simple machine may have only one part. Complex machines have many parts. Some of these parts move. Other parts do not. Complex machines are made of different simple machines working together.

Many of Leonardo's machines were complex machines. He got his ideas from simple machines that had already been invented. The simple machines he used in his drawings are still used in complex machines today.

Archimedes' Screw

People used to carry water from one place to another. This was hard work. It took a long time.

Archimedes was a man who lived long ago in Greece. He invented a simple machine that could move water up from a river or stream. This made life easier for many people. They could get the water they needed without having to carry it themselves.

The machine was called Archimedes' screw. It was an important invention. Some machines today still move water in much the same way. Leonardo knew about Archimedes' screw. People in Europe had been using it for a long time.

Leonardo studied the machines he saw. He drew pictures of them. He thought of ways to make the machines work better. He thought of a way to improve Archimedes' screw.

Leonardo invented a new machine for lifting water. His machine used two screws and a water wheel. Water moved through the water wheel and turned it. The turning wheel turned the screws. The screws lifted the water. Leonardo's water lift could fill a tall water tower. The water flowed down from the tower to places where people needed water.

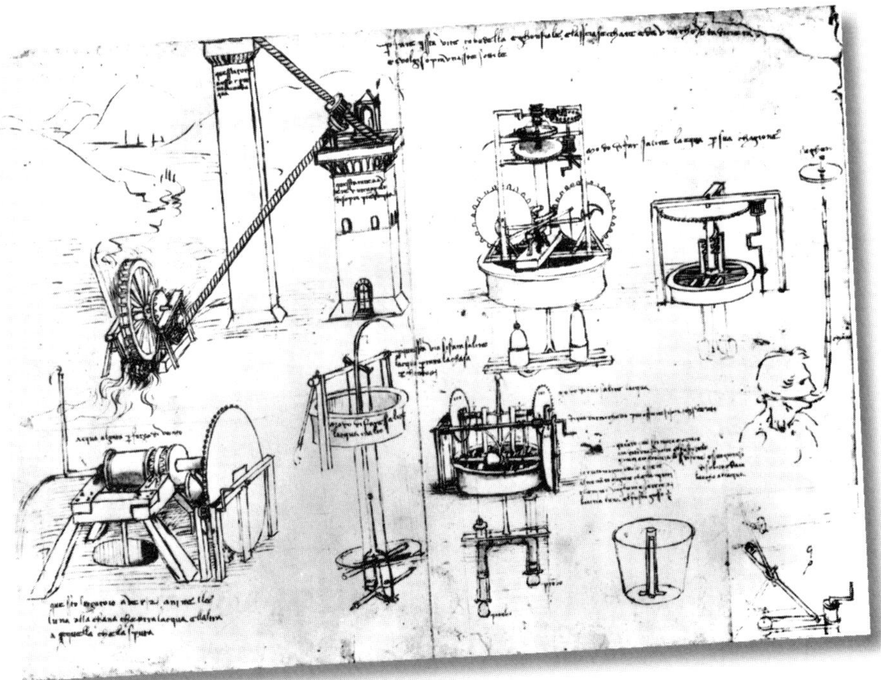

Leonardo improved Archimedes' screw and invented a water lift.

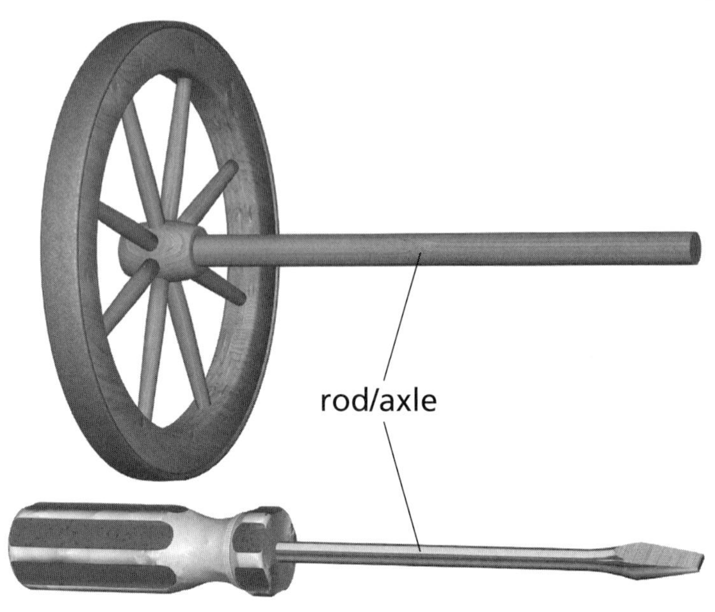

The screwdriver's wide handle increases the force, or effort, you use to turn it.

Wheel and Axle

A screwdriver is a simple tool. Its handle is thicker than its bottom part. A person turns the handle. The bottom part of the screwdriver turns the screw. Turning the handle is easier than trying to turn the screw with your fingers.

The screwdriver is based on a very old simple tool called the wheel and axle. An axle is a rod in the middle of a wheel. An axle can connect two wheels together. Wagons use wheels and axles. It is easier to pull something heavy in a wagon than to carry it.

Many complex machines use wheels and axles to make it easier to move things. Leonardo used wheels and axles in some of his machines.

During Leonardo's time, people often used boats to get from place to place. The boats traveled along rivers and canals. Sometimes large amounts of mud flowed into the rivers and canals. The boats could not pass through.

Leonardo invented a machine to help clear the mud from rivers and canals. The wheel and axle made it easier to move a lot of mud.

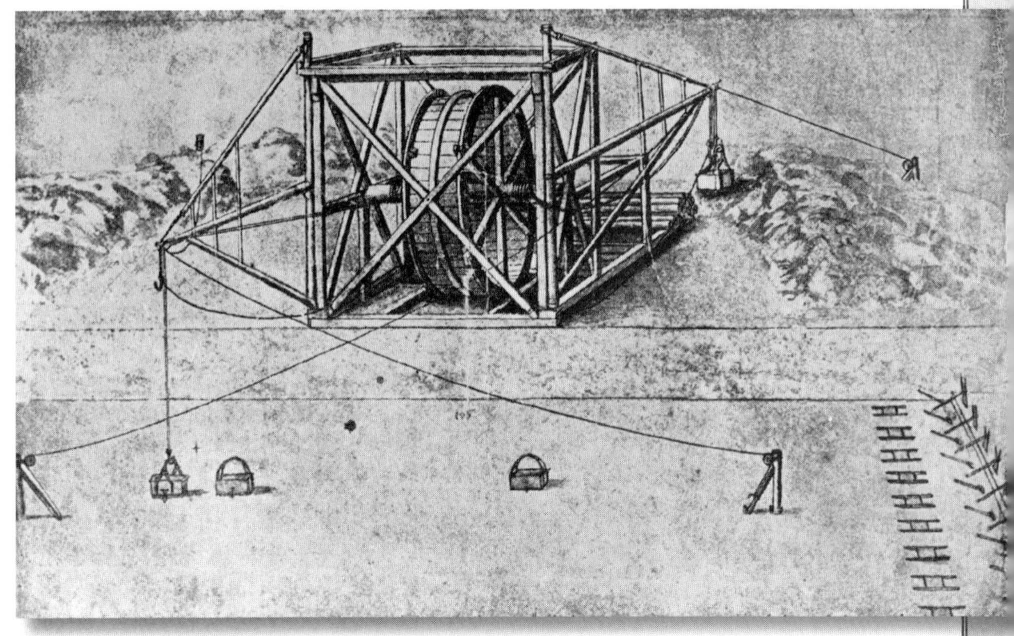

This is Leonardo's drawing of a machine to scrape the bottom of rivers and canals.

Pulley

A pulley is a wheel with a groove. A groove is a thin cut made around the wheel. A rope or chain slides along the groove. The groove keeps the rope or chain from sliding off. Pulling down on one end of the rope or chain lifts the object attached to the other end.

A pulley is a simple machine. It helps people lift heavy things. Using a pulley to lift something is easier than trying to lift it yourself.

Some pulleys have more than one wheel. More wheels make it even easier to lift very heavy things. More wheels mean you need to pull the rope or chain a long distance. The object attached to the other end is lifted only a short distance. It feels as though the weight is much less. Someone who is not very strong can use pulleys to lift something very heavy.

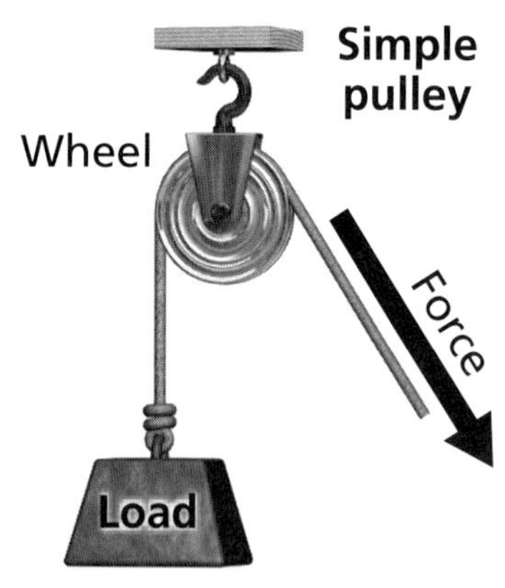

A simple pulley has one wheel.

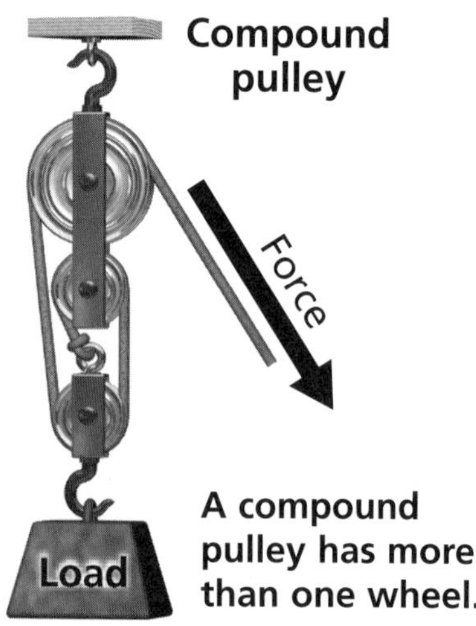

A compound pulley has more than one wheel.

Compare Leonardo's drawing of a crane to this photo of a crane used today.

A crane uses pulleys to help lift heavy things. Long ago, cranes used pulleys to help lift large stones for building. Today, cranes use pulleys to help build tall buildings.

Leonardo did not invent the crane. People were already using cranes before he was born. What Leonardo did was invent ways to make cranes better. There are many drawings of cranes in his notebooks.

Lever

A lever is another simple machine. A crowbar is a type of lever. People use crowbars to push heavy rocks out of the ground. It is easier than trying to lift the rock. Levers, like pulleys, change the direction of the force, or effort. For example, if you push down on a lever, the object lifts up.

It is easy to use a crowbar. You place one end under an object. Then you press down on the other end of the crowbar. The end you push on moves down. The heavy object moves up. You need to keep pressing down for a long time to lift something heavy. The longer you push, the stronger the force is.

People use levers every day. A clothespin is a lever. A baseball bat is a lever, too. A wheelbarrow uses both a lever and a wheel and axle. Even a piano uses levers.

This boy uses a crowbar to lift the rock.

Leonardo used levers in his plans to make a better printing press. A printing press is a machine that prints books and papers. The first printing press had already been invented. Once again, Leonardo was trying to make something better. He used levers to make the machine work faster.

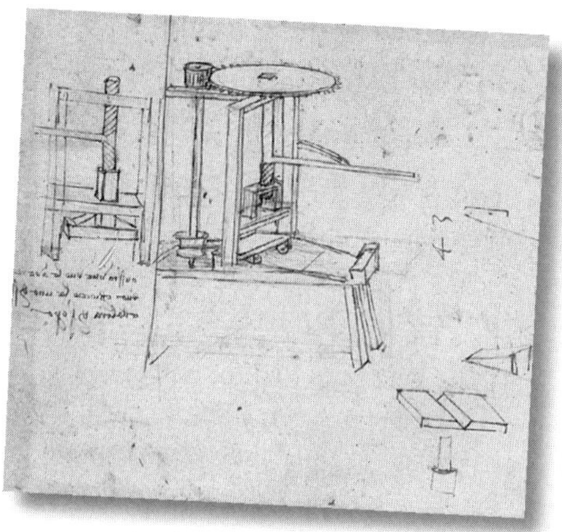

A printing press with a page-feeder

Leonardo also used levers in his plans for clocks. Clocks had already been invented. However, people knew how to build only very big clocks. They often broke. Leonardo drew many pictures of clocks. He studied all the parts. He invented an alarm clock. His alarm clock did not use a loud sound to wake someone up. Instead, water flowed through the clock and, at the right time, lifted the person's feet into the air!

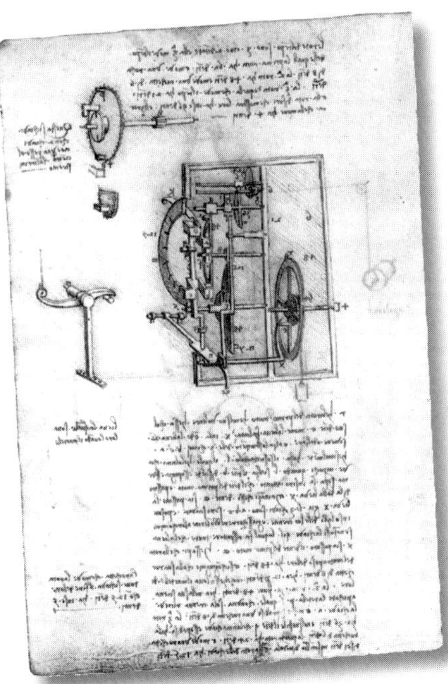

A drawing of a clock

Flying Machines

Leonardo spent many years trying to invent a way for people to fly. At that time, there were no airplanes. People did not understand how flight was possible. Leonardo studied birds. He studied bats, too. He thought their wings allowed them to fly.

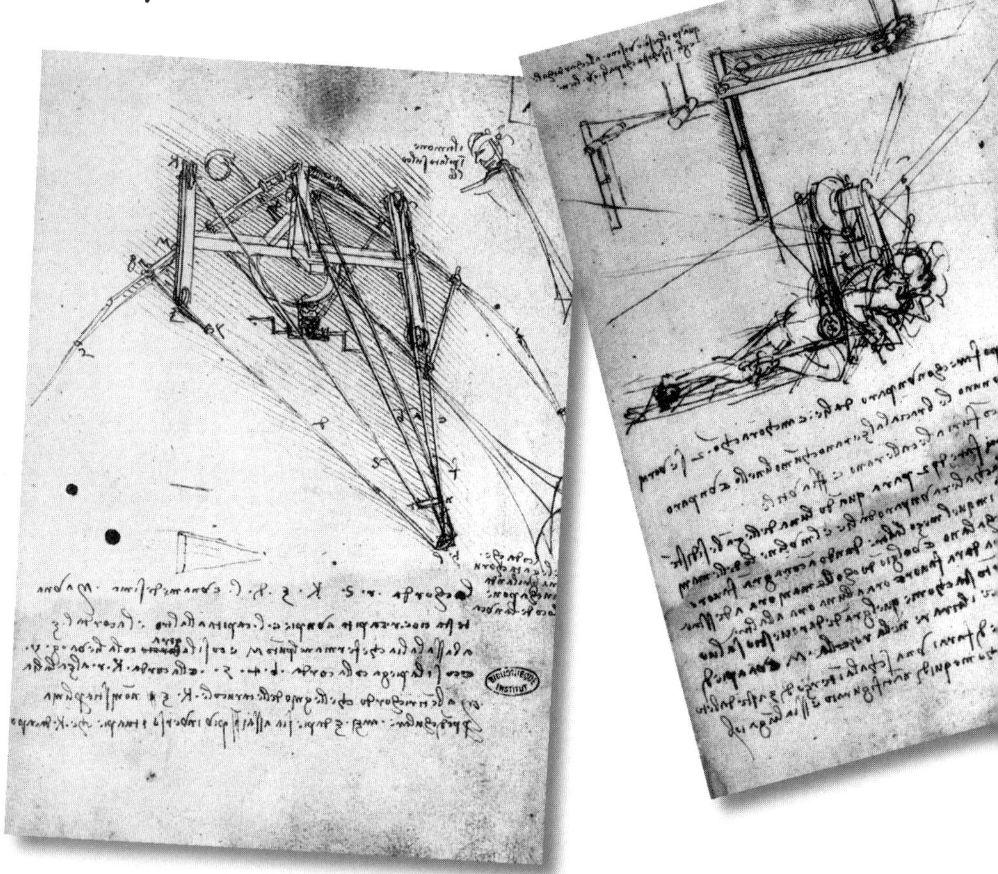

Leonardo made many drawings of flying machines.

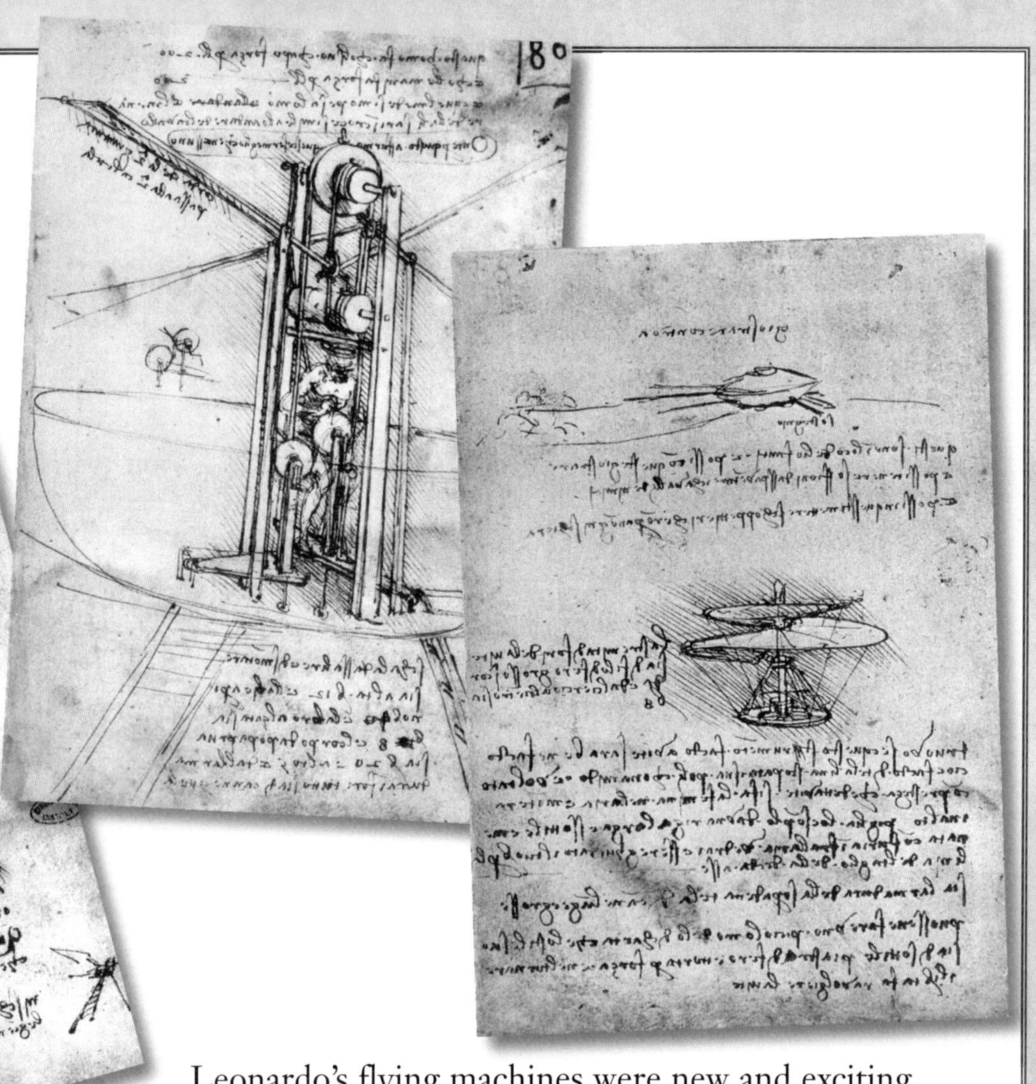

Leonardo's flying machines were new and exciting. However, they were missing something very important: engines. Engines have power. They have many parts. Engines move machines such as cars, airplanes, and lawnmowers. Leonardo did not know how to make an engine to move his flying machines.

Most of Leonardo's machines were never built. They are only drawings. He may have made small examples called models of some of his machines. These models have not been found.

Leonardo did not have the money to build his machines. He showed his drawings to kings and other important people. He hoped they would give him the money he needed.

Leonardo drew a design for a parachute.

There were other reasons Leonardo could not build his machines. His ideas were very modern. It would have been hard for him to find the parts he needed to build many of his machines.

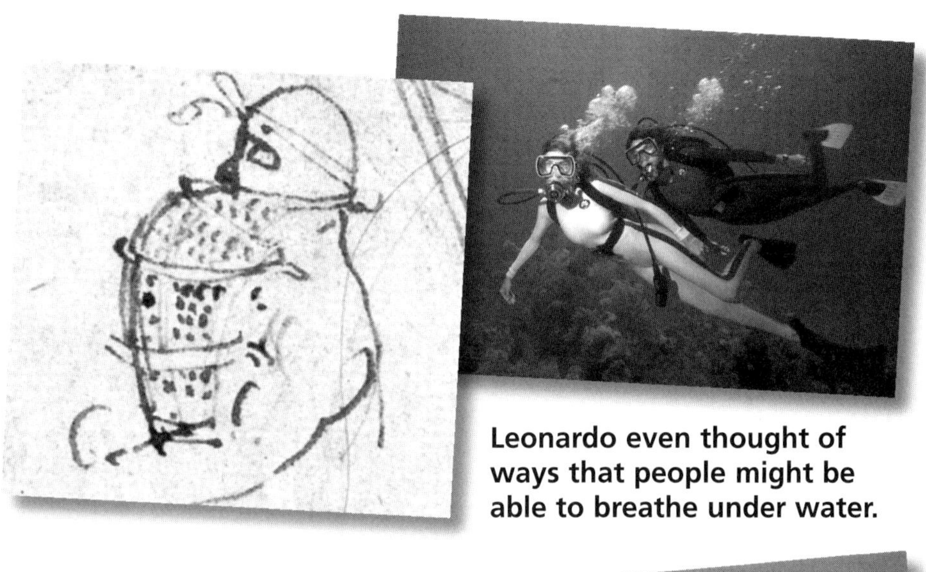

Leonardo even thought of ways that people might be able to breathe under water.

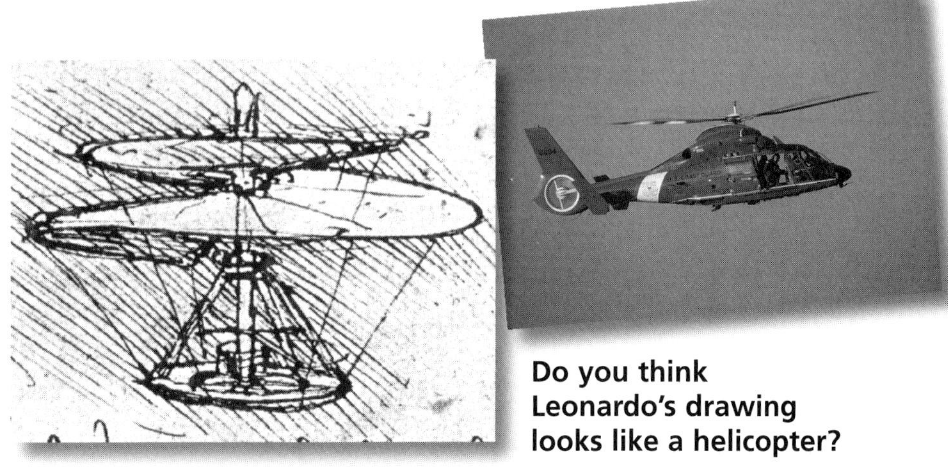

Do you think Leonardo's drawing looks like a helicopter?

Leonardo's notebooks are written in a strange way. Leonardo wrote backwards, from right to left. He wrote with his left hand. Maybe he found it easier to write this way. Sometimes Leonardo wrote in a secret code. Maybe he did not think other people would understand his work or use it wisely.

Leonardo drew many pictures of machines he invented himself. He could not draw in code. Instead, Leonardo put mistakes in his drawings. He made these mistakes on purpose. He did not want other people to be able to make the things he drew.

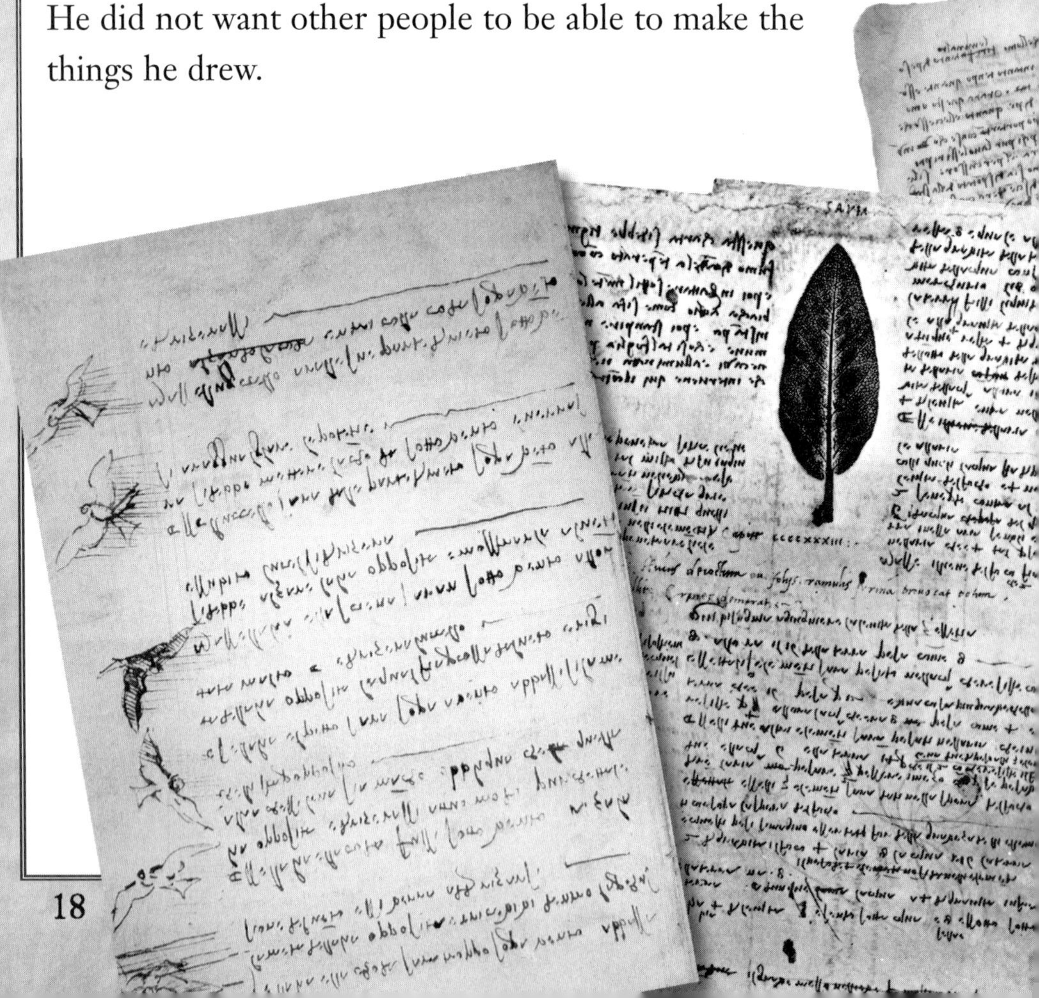

Leonardo died hundreds of years ago, but people are still trying to build some of his machines. They use modern equipment. They can make all the parts. Some of Leonardo's machines work, and some do not.

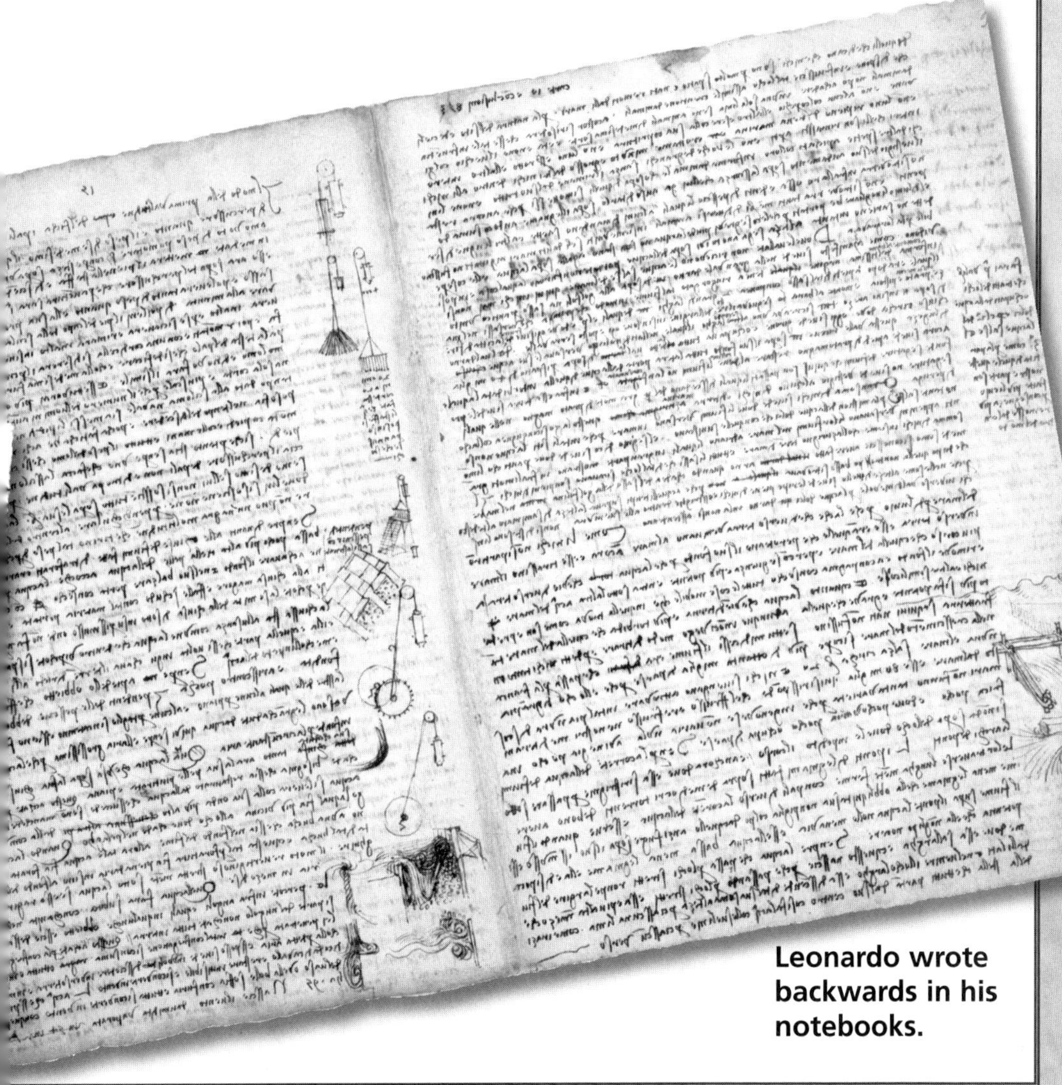

Leonardo wrote backwards in his notebooks.

ACTIVITY: Make a Wheel and Axle

Materials:

Screw

Screwdriver

Piece of wood

Spool

2 Pencils

Paper

Place the screw point down on the wood.
Try to turn the screw into the wood with your hands.
Now, use the screwdriver to turn the screw.
Which way is easier?

A screwdriver is an example of a wheel and axle.

You can make your own wheel and axle using a spool and a pencil.
Slide the spool onto the sharp end of the pencil. Make sure it is on tight. The spool and pencil should move together as one.

The spool is the wheel. The pencil is the axle. It looks a little like a screwdriver. The spool is like the handle.

The following experiment will show you why it is easier to turn a screw using a screwdriver.

Step 1: Take apart the spool and pencil.
Draw a dot on the edge of the spool.
Draw a dot on a sheet of paper.
Line up the two dots.
Roll the spool until its dot touches the paper again.
Mark this spot with another dot.
The distance between the two dots on the paper is equal to one full turn of the spool.
The spool rolls a long distance in one turn.

Step 2: Make a dot on the side of your pencil.
Line it up with the first dot on the paper.
Roll the pencil until its dot touches the paper again.
Mark this spot with another dot.
The pencil rolled a much shorter distance than the spool.

This simple machine exchanges distance for effort. That means that the wheel turns a greater distance than the axle. This makes the force stronger. That's why it's easier to turn a screw using a screwdriver (wheel and axle).

Events in Leonardo's Life

April 15, 1452 Born near Florence, Italy, probably near the town of Vinci.

1460s As a teenager, became an apprentice to Andrea del Verrochio, a sculptor and painter in Florence.

About 1478 Had his own artist studio in Florence.

1482 Became court artist for the Duke of Milan. Leonardo also designed locks for the canals in Milan, Italy; stages for the city's pageants; and fortresses for the military.

1500 Returned to Florence.

1513 The Pope invites Leonardo to stay in the Vatican in Rome.

1516 King of France invites Leonardo to be the official painter, engineer, and architect of the king.

May 2, 1519 Dies in France.

Glossary

Archimedes' screw a simple machine for lifting water

complex machine a machine with many moving parts

engine a complex machine for powering other machines

lever a simple machine, like a crowbar, for lifting something

machine something with moving and non-moving parts that makes work easier

pulley a simple machine with a grooved wheel and a rope or chain

simple machine a machine with only a few moving parts that requires less force for a longer distance to perform a task

wheel and axle a simple machine made from a rod (axle) and one or more wheels

Index